LIFE TIDES

MEDITATIONS BY
ELIZABETH TARBOX

Boston
Skinner House Books

Printed in the USA.

Design by Suzanne Morgan

Project Editor: Brenda Wong

10 9 8 7 6 5 4 3 2 1
99 98 97 96 95 94 93 92

Acknowledgment
Excerpt from *The Prophet* by Kahlil Gibran, copyright 1923 by Kahlil Gibran and renewed 1951 by Administrators C.T.A. of Kahlil Gibran Estate and Mary G. Gibran, reprinted by permission of Alfred A. Knopf, Inc.

Tarbox, Elizabeth, 1944-
    Life tides : meditations / by Elizabeth Tarbox.
       p. cm.
    ISBN 1-55896-307-3
      1. Meditations. 2. Spiritual life—Unitarian Universalist authors. I. Title.
BV4832.2.T37 1992
242—dc20

92-33384
CIP

CONTENTS

To

Charles Tarbox

and

Sarah Tarbox

I thank Robbie Walsh, Dick Fewkes, Valerie Peck, and John Cole for their assistance, support, and encouragement; and I thank the congregations of the First Parish Church in Duxbury, the First Parish of Norwell, and the First Unitarian Universalist Society of Middleborough, MA who taught me about ministry.

PREFACE

I thought I heard the voice of the spirit cry:

Come and find me. You won't have to look hard. Come to where
the ocean touches the shore; find me in the bright-light promise
of morning on the waves; look carefully at the bubbles breaking
on the wet sand—there I am. Turn over the glistening rock,
slippery with its cushion of seaweed—here I am. Hear the gulls
crying news of the endless ocean—that is my news, my voice.
Lie with me in the tall, green marsh grass; see my footprints
in the sand you have walked upon. Do not say I am lost,
for you have found me.
I am here.

ARIZONA SUNRISE

The sun rose over Monument Valley this morning. It was quiet, a quiet you could feel inside, broken occasionally by the greeting of an unknown bird or animal. The red desert dawn hit the rocks and set them alight, tall sentinel rocks pointing to the red and orange sky and to an eternity of waiting.

I was in Monument Valley at sunrise once. It was June 1972. The sun impacted the sky and there were three of us there, watching, touched for one holy moment by the immensity of that sunrise, struck to silence by the presence of the sacred. We are so frail; we share a few moves, a few breaths, our hearts beat to the rhythm of the universe for a moment or two, and we are gone. But the sun rises over Monument Valley each day as it has done for ages before I lived, as it has done all these thousands of mornings since the day I was there, as it will long, long after my footprints are gone from the earth. We live for a time only, but during that time we can, if we choose, find places like Monument Valley at sunrise and stand there and pause in our activity and find an infinite peace, a peace not of our making,
a peace which truly does defy our understanding.
It is there for us; we need only pause
and wait for it to come.

NEW YEAR

It's strange to talk of New Year's resolutions when so little can ever be resolved. Resolving suggests to me completion, packaging, the tying up of loose ends. I'm lucky if I resolve the laundry or tonight's supper; I can never hope to resolve my feelings or my behavior.

The best I can do is to try to write about these feelings that have no name, that crowd each other, bubbling up sometimes like a mountain spring, and more often like a broken fire hydrant. My days are a series of unresolved feelings. With all life has taught me of the cycles of birth and death, the orderliness of the universe, and the arbitrariness of our individual fortunes, there are still moments in almost every day when my weeping voice cries out, "Oh no, don't let this happen." I plead for intercession, for the breaking in of grace, for God to resolve things in my favor.

I experience joy in the wonder of nature and excitement in creativity; I do pause from time to time to let gratitude spill over me, and I keep open the invitation to love. Yet the price for all this openness is an equal measure of fear. The price I pay for loving is the panic of pessimism. The shower of well-being and gratitude is opposed by the slimy mud of jealousy, anger, and bitterness; my appreciation of this exquisite planet brings with it the weight of knowing I am contributing to its ill health with my consumption of its resources and my inattention to its endangered species. Unresolved feelings, prayers which cannot be answered to my satisfaction without breaking the very laws of nature that the Creator took such care to establish.

This year I'm not making resolutions, or asking God to resolve things for me. This year, as I take my self-inventory, I'm aiming

for the continued willingness to keep the doors of my feelings
open, to participate in life as well as to observe it, to contribute
more to the solutions and less to the problems,
and to wish everyone, with all my heart,
a happy and healthy new year.

THE CLOCK

The clock arrived from England this week. It is an ornately carved table clock with a comforting tick that gently marks the quarter- and half-hours and noisily chimes the hours. It has an inscription which reads "Presented to James Usher by the congregation of the Parish Church of Thornaby-on-Tees, as a token of their appreciation of his 31 years of service to the Parish as Churchwarden. Easter 1905."

James Usher was my husband's great-grandfather, but he died before Charles was born. James and Charles never met, but the clock has been a treasured possession of them both. The clock marked the hour of James's death and the birth of his great-grandson. It measured the passage of two world wars and has sustained several house moves. The clock was admired by little children who had to be lifted up to run their curious fingers over its mysterious carvings; later it watched as those children, now grown to beautiful young men and women, dressed for their wedding days, and it watched them grow old.

It is a rather fine clock, but that is not the reason why it is so welcome in our home. It is welcome because it has always been there; in its grain lie the memories of generations, in its crevices hides the dust of history. It is possible that this clock will stand in the sideboard in the homes of great-grandchildren we shall never live to meet. Its lines are as hard and exact as they ever were, while the lines on the faces of the people who take care of it grow deeper and more wrinkly. Why, oh why, should this object, beautiful though it is, live on when dear ones we have loved pass away?

The clock is not alive and we are. That is why. The clock is condemned, like the Flying Dutchman, to survive generations, marking time without ever being able to participate in it. We are short-lived, but we can use time. We can be alive and busy, making, changing, and moving the world in the direction we want it to go. The clock may know things through its years of watching, but its wisdom cannot be passed along. Our structure is less perfect, less enduring, but our knowledge (should we acquire it) can be shaped and tested and offered to the next generation.

The clock has come to us from a time we never knew, and it will move without us into an age we will have created but will not experience. It reminds me that I had better hurry to do my part of the world's work.

KALEIDOSCOPE

Through a kaleidoscope the world becomes fractured, divided twenty-four ways in symmetrical pieces. A single candle flame becomes twenty-four flickering candles, each a perfect replica of the other. The mundane is made exquisite when it is placed in a pattern of identical squares; the ordinary becomes the mystical when it is seen through a prism.

Is this how life is, if only we step back far enough to see it all— a kaleidoscope of events joining, merging, dancing in rhythmic harmony? Could we appreciate the order of life, if we were not one of the fragments? But we are in it, of it, not observers of the pattern but part of the very texture of which it is constructed.

There may be a plan, but we will never be able to stand back far enough to appreciate it. Somewhere life may make sense to a great cosmic someone, but not to us here; not to us, splintered in a struggle to do what is right in a world that presents us with complex, competing options. We may never see the larger picture, creation's perfected whole; we may be forever flickering fragments, fractured by the raw reality of immediacy from which there is no escape while we are alive.

Well then, let us dance in the flame that we see. Let the arc of our creativity embrace our moments of time, and let us add our light to the kaleidoscope, trusting in the unity of the whole even as we seek symmetry with the part.

CROWS

I think if I were not a person, I should like to be a bird, and of them all, I should like to be a crow. Crows are big, strutting, powerful birds, gleaming in the right light and not ashamed of the work they do. But I like them most for the way they circle the tall trees and for the way they cry.

I appreciate most those creatures who know how to cry well, and crows do. Catch them at dawn in their ritual grieving, flying over the tall trees, and you'll hear all the sorrow of your heart wrung out and laid before you.

Crows. All my days there have been crows. As a child I awoke to the crying of crows over the neighbor's oak tree, and when I came to America the crows were already here. Buffleheads and egrets are the delight of my bike rides to the beach, but they are still strangers to me, and we are shy and nervous with each other.
But the archetypal crow is the cousin of my soul;
I long to fly above the maple trees
and cry like a crow.

GOD'S WORK

What is God's work? If God is immanent and transcendent, in and out of everything, then how could it be possible not to do God's work? Surely all work is God's work—there is nothing which is not of God. Is there?

But that doesn't do it, somehow. There are times when what I do is strictly for me. God or no God, I'm working for myself, even during those times when God would probably approve. Mostly what I do for myself is compatible with what I believe I would do for God.

But not always. There are times of conflict, when the prompting and urging of my desire are up against the sentinel of my conscience. They square off, these two strong voices somewhere deep in the thick of me where there is no judge, no referee, and mercifully no spectators. "Do it," say I. "Don't," says God. One of them wins and the other goes grumbling away, threatening and complaining in the basement of my being like a boiler with an excess of steam. And I am left to live with my decision, to forgive or applaud, to bask in my nobility or blush in my shame. And God and I make peace once more.

Then there are times when I can't tell which is God's voice and which is my own. What about those times when God seems to be saying "Do it" and I am saying "No." When God says, "This is the right thing to do," and I, shaking with fear, confess, "I can't, I'm just too scared."

"I'll be with you."

"How do I know?"

"You can do it, be not afraid."

"I might fail, make a fool of myself."

"Yes, you might. Do it anyway."

"But people might not like me."

"That's right."

"But how do I know this is good? How can I be sure?"

"You cannot be sure. This is a risk."

Yes, those are the toughest times: wanting to do right without losing my safety, not knowing if I am doing God's work, or using God to do mine. There is no superhighway named Right Way. There are no signposts, no guides, no promises, no guarantees; only the lonely voice of conscience and the cringing cry of fear wrestling each other in inner space. Those are the times of lying awake at night and staring at the detail of the day through a haze of worry, working and reworking the "oughts," the "shoulds," and the "yes, buts" of the thing.

And what's to be done, but to listen to the voice that seems to
be speaking a consistent truth, move through the fear to
trust the moral judgments we have lived by,
and pray for courage.

EULOGY FOR A LITTLE LAB MAMMAL

Natalie was a gold-and-white guinea pig, with full lips and an overstated stomach. She shared her life with us, accepted our love and care, nibbled daintily on spinach and dandelion, and swooned over the very smell of strawberries. Natalie cherished her mate, Frank, and let us stroke their babies, and forgave us when we gave the babies away.

When Natalie became sick, we took her to the veterinarian and were told that not much could be done for little lab mammals. We were told Natalie would not get well again, so we made that choice which we human animals have granted ourselves and asked the doctor to put her to sleep. But Natalie didn't sleep. She lay in my lap and quivered and sighed, and the life that she had so generously shared with us left her little round body, and she was dead.

And I thought how curious it is that this small animal should move me so; that this little life whose whole span had been but five years should make me wrestle with my conscience about the rights of humans to have charge over animals; how strange that the now still body of this lifeless creature should bring me to tears.

I had personified a guinea pig. I had granted her a place and dignity in my home. By my love I had somehow elevated her to something more than a species of rodent. But she in turn had dignified me by accepting my care. She had brought beauty into our home and had stirred in me emotions I am glad to have—love and the desire to nurture. She had trusted me, thereby making me trustworthy.

Great God, make us friends of the animals. Make us responsible co-inhabitants of this fruitful planet. In our dealings with animals may we be generous; may we exercise our power with compassion and avoid brutality. May we never debase them. May we never use their flesh or their skins wastefully to enhance our appearance. May we respect their right to a good life in their own habitat. In our dealings with animals may we remember that all life is mysterious, precious, and God-given, and that we are honored and blessed by their presence among us.

MOMENT OF SPIRIT

I have this living image in my mind of the moonlight over the water—a broad highway of the most delicate iridescent light fluidly inviting my participation. It calls and I almost follow; nothing matters but the pull of the moon, and my spirit stretches out for it. Mana, let my spirit soar; for once let my soul go free so I may kiss the moon and become the clouds and roll over the ocean.

But the earth clings to my feet with an insistence that cannot be denied. All I can do is sigh and lean into the music of the moon, and imagine my spirit ghostly and gossamer sliding into the silver night. Then I notice on the edge of the cliff in front of me a single tall blade of grass, leaning likewise and dancing to the same call. We are the earthbound ones, left to keep our adventurous spirits longing and leaning, looking for the light.
Keep us poised thus, dear spirit, entrusted
to the earth and moving to the
poetry of the stars.

STORM WATCH

I was hurting so I went to the beach—the icy beach with sand pitted by near-frozen spray from an ocean that roared and rolled and drove a million pebbles before it.

I hardly noticed the Turner sky and the lonely beauty of the Gurnet, for the tears on my cheeks were part wind-wrought and part anger at the unfairness of a world where good people suffer, children are hungry, and no one counts the tears. "Tell me what to do!" I cried, but my voice was thin, and the words froze in the wind and fell lifeless to the sand.

Then I saw the gulls, two or three, here and there, with that gray-flecked look of fledglings, and I wondered how they survived the brutality of a winter no one warned them would be coming. But gulls ride the waves and face into the wind. They ride each wave as it comes—that is how they do it. It is the only way.

If we follow their example, we will ride the waves, take each new challenge, and face it so we can see what is coming and prepare ourselves. If we stay together and face the wind, we may be able to ride out this storm and the next, until the wind stops roaring and the waves become calm. For all its noise and threat, the ocean encroaches only a few yards up the beach each day before it retreats. If we ride the waves and face the wind, we shall still be together tomorrow when the storm is over and the ocean is quiet.

MOTHER'S DAY

Your children are not your children.
They are the sons and daughters of Life's longing for itself.
They come through you but not from you,
And though they are with you yet they belong not to you.
                                        —*The Prophet* by Kahlil Gibran

Though my child belongs not to me, she is my child and always will be.

I watched her running up the driveway on that second day of school, bouncing along in white ankle socks and Stride Rite sandals and a summer dress hand-sewn by an English grandma. I watched her at eight and nine, two yellow braids and a Cookie Monster lunch box. I dropped what I was doing and ran out to meet the bus, in those days when she was little enough to be swept up in my arms and unembarrassed by my affection.

I watched her carrying a trombone case and a school bag that just gets heavier, trudging up that driveway on cold winter mornings in junior high when no one wore a winter jacket or socks, no matter how much snow covered the yard. I watched her just last week when her boyfriend came to meet her in his car, and they walked out together arm in arm, he carrying the trombone case. Then, when I watched her asking questions of the admissions officer at a liberal arts college, I knew that I could count the number of days I have left to watch her from the window.

Spirit of life, watch my child when I cannot. Encircle her with love, protect her from a world which has become cynical. Knowing that I cannot stop time, not even for a moment, and freeze the picture of her from my window, let me hold her gently in my memory. Let all those children she once was remain joyful spirits enriching my reminiscences. Spirit of life, watch all our children. Keep them safe as they adventure toward adulthood, and let them turn and wave to us as they step out of our care and into the world of their making.

SUFFICIENCY

There is a limit to how much awe I can feel, even when I'm standing on a beach at dawn with all that religion means to me rolled out before my wondering eyes.

There is a limit to my acquisitiveness: I have more than enough stuff now. I have all the things I could possibly want to make my life comfortable. I have plenty of belongings, thank you.

But love, O God, there is no limit to my longing for love. Love is so elusive and so precious and doesn't follow any rules. I can't make people love me, or keep their love once I have it, or invest it in the bond market and draw on the interest. I can't catch love in a bottle and look at it in the afternoon when I'm lonely. I can't get love on demand with a bank card.

Knowing that love is not a limited resource, not an endangered species, doesn't help at all. What does it matter if there is a vast ocean of love out there, if I'm not able to immerse myself in it; if I'm locked up in here, without a drop of that ocean's moisture to bless me?

Here's what I can do. I can be open to the possibility of love. I can recognize love when it's offered. I can be vulnerable, knowing that those who dare not risk giving are unable to receive. I can admit that being loved is an exercise in letting go, in surrendering control, in being humbly grateful for what is given.

I can accept love and let even the smallest amount of it grow in me and shine out of me. I can say at last: "The love that you give me is very good, and it is enough."

BETWEEN SEASONS

Tiny sparkles from diamond drops of ice high up in the naked branches of the maple and elm reflect the sun through my window and work at distracting me.

Beneath their frozen coats, the tiny buds of spring wait to be born, but winter has one last picture to show me before spring comes laughing to the trees. As if they were working together in this month between seasons—sunshine, catbirds, and crocuses for spring, and icicles hanging on pine needles and cardinals picking sunflower seeds off the snow-drifted bird feeder for winter—the two seasons call forth from me a great Amen.

Here we are then, between seasons, not knowing for sure what to do next. Do we conserve and play it safe against an unexpected onslaught striking us like one last winter blast, or do we cast off our coats and take a risk, daring to embrace a spring which is not quite here? Thank God we have each other and this place of worship to come to, when we need to make decisions in our search for both security and renewal. May we remember in the chilliest winter storm or the balmiest spring morning that
this place is here for us, that here we share in
creation's love no matter what
the season.

THE HEALING MOMENT

Each day I am newly reminded of my unworthiness: a dozen thoughts misspoken; another day when the good I do falls so far short of the good that I could do; myriad small interchanges, moments of sharing that strain to the breaking point my desire to be generous, helpful, and kind; months of careful work lost by a moment's impatience, a careless word.

But when I am here at the edge of creation, breaking with the small tide over the sand, the need to do good rolls away; the question of what is right diminishes to insignificance and is easily borne away by the tiny waves. Here, where no words are spoken, none are misspoken.

I am with the broken stubble of the marsh grass that holds on through the wrecking wind and the burning flood. I am with the grains that mold themselves around everything, accepting even so unworthy a foot as mine, holding and shaping it until it feels that it belongs. I stand somewhere between truth and vision, and what I don't know ceases to embarrass me, because what I do know is that the water feels gentle like a lover's touch, and the sand welcomes it.

What I have done or failed to do has left no noticeable mark on creation. What I do or don't do is of no moment now. Now I am here and grateful to be touched, calmed, and healed by the immense pattern of the universe. And when I die, it will be an honor for my blood to return to the sea and my bones to become the sand.

Reassured, I am called back to my life, to another day.

MARSUPIAL SHELL

The shell on my desk is long and rolled up. I don't know its name or where it came from, only that it is here, and beautiful biscuit shades wave over it in perfect parallel lines. Within its folds nestle two other tiny round shells. They are safe there, protected.

How we long to stay in the firm grasp of someone else's arms, to be swept up in their adventure and protected like these fragile twins in the shell's embrace, to be cared for, to be encircled, to sleep secure.

But there is another way of seeing the ocean's artwork. Those little shells are stuck. Somehow, sometime, they were washed inside the other's grip and nothing, neither the action of the ocean nor the roughness of the beach upon which the family foundered, can set them free without breaking the shell which protects them. As long as they remain as they are, they will not grow.

Perhaps we are like the shells, wanting as parents to hold on to those for whom we feel responsible; wanting our babies not to take on the uncertainty of life alone. But I believe that relationships were not meant to be as rigid or confining as the sculpture of these three shells. We are swept up in the open ocean of adulthood, formed by the elements of work and play, shaped by the holding on and the letting go, smoothed and wrinkled by saying hello and saying good-bye. Each of us deserves a separate, special life, with love enough to protect but not disfigure us.

Creator Spirit, grant us the strength to know when to hold on to our dear ones and when to let them go; provide us the protection of loving arms which give us the security to choose our freedom; and when we come to rest at last, let it be in the calm of some safe harbor.

FATHER'S DAY

Creator, whom some call Father, we are gathered here to worship together on a day set aside to recognize and praise all fathers. It is easy, God, to thank our perfect father, the one who was unfailingly wise and kind, who worked hard all day and still had time to play baseball or take us out for ice cream in the evening. We are eager to thank the father who showed us by example what responsible citizenship is, who laughed and cried with us as he read us our bedtime story, who shared his problems with us and trusted us with his feelings, who set us firmly on the road to adulthood and knew just when to hug us close and when to let us go.

But we have a harder time knowing what to say to our imperfect father, the one who struggled and fell short or didn't seem to care at all. There are no cards to tell the father who treated us unkindly that the wound is still open. We are hardly granted permission on Father's Day, or at any other time, to tell our father that we really wanted to love him but he wouldn't let us get that close, or that we really wanted his love but he hurt us instead.

God, today, grant us a measure of peace with our memories and our feelings. If there can be reconciliation with our imperfect father, honesty, forgiveness, and healing, then let it be so; but if that is not possible, then at least let us find peace with ourselves. Let part of our maturity be the acceptance of the reality that father-son and father-daughter relationships can be destructive, and that it is not our fault. If our father was or is a source of discomfort to us, then let us know that that is a truth which may not be changed. We cannot change our father; we can only change ourselves, and then only after we have understood the truth and grieved over our hurts.

So God, today, bless our fathers—all of them. Lead us to a true appreciation of their qualities and a recognition of their frailties. Let us stop expecting more than our fathers can give and start giving what we can to them. And let us remember that we can learn how to parent from all the examples shown to us, the good and the bad.

LOVE SONGS

When I was a child, there was a singer named Carl Brissom who may have been from Denmark. He was a smooth baritone, singing the songs of the thirties and forties, and he died before I had hardly begun to live. But my mother loved him and used to sigh, and sing along, and smile or weep when his songs were played on the radio. He always wore a gardenia in his lapel, she told me, and I used to laugh at my mother's love for him and tease her about her tears.

Why would I think of that now, so many years after the deaths of both of them? One night during the summer, I watched a videotape of an old Marlene Dietrich concert staged at the now-closed theater in Golders Green, London. I had seen her there in 1966, heard her songs, and watched her ethereal figure. It remains one of the most outstanding theatrical experiences of my life: her slim outline in white and silver commanding the love and awed attention of her audience. I was twenty-two then, and as well as being entranced by her performance I was amused by the emotions of many people around me. Men in their fifties and sixties were throwing roses and cheering with tears in their eyes and trembling lips, and perhaps I was embarrassed by the sentimentality.

But now, years later, I am not laughing. Now I am silenced by Marlene Dietrich singing her songs of passionate commitment to peace among nations and people. I know now that her songs reminded those men of days when war tore at the gentle security of their young lives, when love and war were juxtaposed and nothing made sense, and only comradeship counted.

Now I wish I hadn't laughed at my mother who loved Carl
Brissom. I wish I could tell her that I was humbled by time,
and now I'm appreciative of people who
can be moved to tears
by a song.

WORDS

Let's keep talking, my love. Words we have to spare: love words and angry words, and beneath them hurting, bleeding, dying words, and beneath them words melted by fire and hardened by ice, words of sadness and truth birthed from the cavern of tears.

And when the words are spent, heaped over the pages and spilled to the floor, let us read each other's eyes and see the chapters and the places where old bookmarks press the pages apart, so the book opens up to the old story before we can move on.

For you are all the love words I have ever heard and all the hurt words where the love is deepest, stripped back and bleeding.

But let's keep caring, ever so slowly building down the words, one beneath the other, getting closer to the truth and still deeper until you touch your words to my wounds, honor them, and feel the pain. Our wounds may not be healed by the touch of the other's words but are dignified by our recognition of their existence.

Then and only then will the words mean anything; when we have used them up until the old meanings have been scrubbed off; when the wrong words have been tried and discarded and the right words have been spoken in a whisper, then let us climb down into each other's soul and rest there in the silence, and love.

THE SURVIVOR

There is a boat lying in the mud at Shipyard Lane at low tide. Its hull is cracked, and small sea creatures cling to its sides.

It has been there a long time, rustily chained to a weathered buoy. But this is no ancient fishing craft, drowned in a North Atlantic storm or torn apart in the freezing airborne ice off Cape Horn. This is a fiberglass boat, painted bright sky blue, built for the cocky, careless youths of summer to show off their sailing skills. It must have watched them leave, the easy-going boys and girls, and waited for the next afternoon and the next, when they would hoist its colored sail and zip across the bay. But they never came back, and summer turned to fall, and all the other boats were hauled resisting from the water and stowed in winter berths until only this one was left, bobbing about on fine fall days and pulling at its chain.

The mast came down in the first November blast and lay for a while across the sky-blue hull. On frigid winter days and in drenching February rains, the boat was there. I don't know when the cracks appeared or when the wooden seat broke loose and floated away. But sometime in March it didn't rise with the tide, and today it lies broken in spite of the fresh June sunshine and easy breeze. I don't believe it is looking for summer youths now. It has stopped longing for expert young hands and rope-soled sandals. They may come back, but the boat won't be waiting for them. She is just visible above the water; she belongs to the time-honored wreckage of the ocean; now she is the sister of the Titanic.

THE UNACCOMPANIED MILE

"Where were you when I laid the foundation of the earth?" said God to Job. "Have you commanded the morning since your days began, and caused the dawn to know its place?"

—*Job* 38:4

When I see you with worry on your brow and shadows in your eyes, and I say to you "What's up?" remind me gently that I was not there when you made that journey to the center of your soul. Tell me as kindly as you can that I am sleeping when night clutches at you and you are driven to a place in your heart which is ever night. Do not let me say "Don't worry," when worry is all you know and it feels as if worry is all you'll ever know.

For none of us ever really walks in another's shoes or knows the innermost rooms of a person's heart. None of us truly knows the lonely places of another's journey or the causes of the lines around another's eyes. Therefore, let us be gentle with one another. Let us listen more than we speak and accept more than we judge. Let our open, outstretched hands reach and touch that we may walk along together for a little while in friendship and in trust.

APPROACH TO SUMMER

Summer is an article of faith: faith in beaches and barbecues and suntan oil. We know that Thanksgiving will come because the calendar says so, and Christmas will never pass unnoticed while the free enterprise system is in place, but summer cannot be legislated by elected officials or defined by toy manufacturers.

Faith in the coming summer begins when we prune our roses in October or plant peas in March before the snow has quite cleared. It is upheld when we tell our employers in January that we want the first two weeks in August off and make an airline reservation for Zurich or book a campsite in Acadia.

For me summer is cycling and the smell of hot pine needles. It is wading carefully into the unaccustomed ocean and feeling the contrast between the chill of my feet and legs and the warmth of the sun on my shoulders, and the awareness of my vulnerability in the hugeness of this liquid world. Summer is a week with my family at Star Island, a magic place that reappears for me each July like some sunbaked and seagull-nested Brigadoon.

Summer is truly an article of faith and an act of God. I pray that your summer will be what you want most from the season. I wish for you warm breezes if you sail, high breakers if you surf, an unlimited supply of No. 30 sun block if you bask, and coals that light with one match if you barbecue. I wish for you an occasional hour with a trashy novel and a butterscotch sundae, and an evening without bug bites. And I wish for you love, conversation, and a summer of joy that matches your memories of what summer should be.

We give thanks for times of recreation. Bless us Spirit of Life
through all the days of our summer and be with us
as we stroll slowly toward September.

GHOST IN THE ORCHARD

When I was little there was an orchard in my life. It belonged to a great-aunt of mine, Auntie Carrie. She was tiny. Even when I was ten I stood head and shoulders above her and looked down on the dainty embroidered cap she wore. She dressed in clothes that reached her ankles and wore narrow black shoes. She lived in a battered-looking cottage which leaked and sagged and smelled of decay. It was a converted summer house in a land not acclaimed for its summers; a little shack embedded in several acres of undergrowth.

Auntie Carrie was dear to me, and loved me and my sister. She understood what magic the orchard held and didn't complain that our visits to her were short in order for our playtime in the orchard to be long. There were apple trees, all higgledy-piggledy, maybe twenty of them, shooting up from grass that grew three feet tall. I suppose the trees had been planted in straight lines, but apple trees know nothing of geometry and by then they were gloriously disarranged, their branches going first one way and then the other, exploring, exploding out and up.

Each of us had a special tree—my sister, our friend Vonny, and me, and various other kids we used to invite over. The name of my tree was Beauty of Bath. Her apples were small, hard, and sweet and had a tough yellowish-orange skin. No one tended the apple trees or any of the fruit that grew in Auntie Carrie's garden. The trees blossomed each year, bore their fruit, and dropped them. No one except us kids harvested any of it.

I knew that my mother had lived there with Auntie Carrie before my folks married, and that was the reason why my father never came over; but in those days I knew my mother the way I knew Florence Nightingale or Queen Victoria—as someone important who had lived a long time ago. To me the apple orchard was anything and everything I wanted it to be, no memories, only adventures on long summer afternoons with my sister and our friends.

That apple orchard was there for all those everlasting years of childhood until Auntie Carrie moved to a nursing home when I was fourteen. She died two years later. She left the property in her will to me and my sister, but we were not consulted about its disposition. People more knowledgeable about such things sold it for us and put the money in a savings account.

Selling that orchard seems like a betrayal now; the apple trees meant more to us than the money ever did. But it's okay; the real value of the place cannot be sold. That's why I got such a pang this morning as I cycled passed a little bit of unkempt grass with
some apple trees growing on it a mile or two from
our home. I hope that apple orchard
has a child in its life.

THE CHANGING SEASON

I watched a man slowly, methodically strain his sailboat out of the water this morning. The boat and the man moved reluctantly, resisting the work. He was marking the inevitable change of seasons, and, as if to remind him that the days of summer were over, the waves suddenly grew irritable and slapped noisily at the streaming wet hull of the little craft.

Lucky are those whose seasons merge together and are greeted by equanimity and even optimism. Lucky are those who can open their arms to changing seasons and changing life, noticing not the chill of encroaching autumn, but the fleeting beauty of a single yellow leaf floating delicately in that patch of ocean so recently occupied by the summer sailboat.

God grant us equal pleasure in the autumn leaves and in the summer's leisure; quicken our senses to the good rich smell of morning earth and evening moisture; tune our hearts to the gentle scrunch of pine needles beneath our shoes, and the industry of squirrels. God give us peace in the changing of our seasons and the autumn of our lives.

FRAGMENT OF FREEDOM

"I saw you at the ocean this morning," you said. I wondered how could you see me since, at the ocean, I am invisible except to the horseshoe crab and the clam. I fade into the salt spray over the raft; I become the business of the crow, the cry of the arctic tern, and the rustle of summer-filled leaves rehearsing the theology of the fall.

How can you see me when I am the gossamer spirit tickling the masts of sleeping sailboats and rolling marbles in the sand? Give me a minute to be off over the ocean, blowing with eternity across the fields of aqueous creation before I have to reappear, solid and responsible, to step into my water-logged sandals and my life.

Give me moments of pure spirit, dear God, and places to play.
Give me spaces of time out of time where all my
incarnations coalesce into one fragment of
freedom, one particle of peace.

CALM SOUL

The calm soul of all things calls to me from the place where the ocean meets the land. I see creation misted over the gentle water, moving along the snow-flecked shore.

I hear creation from the throat of the sea gull and the crow. I see God in the light-bright extravagance of sunrise and the movement of buffleheads rearranging their feathers and watching for the warmth, and I hear God in the gently falling clumps of snow as the winter-wrapped trees give up their gloves for spring.

God crashes over frozen rocks spraying ideas above my head, glinting with morning, too fleeting to catch. God plays at my feet, nudging and hinting and inviting my participation. God is restless and free, moving to the call of the wind. God is that moment when I lose myself to something which is beyond and within me. And somewhere, along the soft edges of the morning, it comes to me that God is a feeling prompted by love.

(Inspired by "Calm Soul of All Things" by Matthew Arnold, in Hymns for the Celebration of Life, Unitarian Universalist Association, Boston.)

AUTUMNAL INVITATION

Dark, dank, moss-covered stones of autumn. Layer upon layer of moldering leaves, decomposing, separating molecules, changing, becoming earth.

There is a fearfulness which infects the fantasies of a lone walker through these leaves, sinking through the season of decay, feeling the inevitability of that invitation to return to the earth. The rain soaks through me, dripping off the trees above, washing me away, back into the fullness of nature's womb. Come, she invites, lie down, rest in me, return to me. Come back.

But life is the interval when we rise up and move against the margin of air, earth, and water. Life is the slow drawing together of our moisture-dipped cells so we can surge with the wind and press against the great sky. I shall walk on for a while yet, stretching toward the stars of my dreams, resisting the pull of the earth while I can still breathe. For there is work to do for human beings, there is love to make, poems to write, and nights of dancing to the moon. There are calls to answer and songs yet to sing, and the earth will wait. She will wait; we will be there soon enough.

A TRILOBITE POET

Two birds call back and forth, echoing a secret not shared with me...

It's one of those moments when my senses are seduced. The ocean flows through my fingers, and I am flooded with the love songs of seabirds; I am the color of sand and the texture of marsh grass.

I tinker with metaphor and alliteration, I fool with mirages and moods. I am a word person. There's a poet buried in me—fossil hard and silent as stone—a trilobite poet who leans out to you, longing to touch your poet and be understood; no clever words, just a leaning out, and a touching and an understanding.

All the poets who have leaned out and taught me what love is are pressed into that fossil poet in me; all the endless eras of waiting and the stomachache fear of disappointment are compressed there. Petrified dreams lie frozen, buried beneath layers of words. It's all there, hardened within the age-old shell of my Paleozoic self, waiting to be exhumed by the call of wild birds fishing the dark ocean, waiting to be touched and warmed by the silent poet in you.

INVOCATION

The leaves abandon themselves to the metamorphosis of the
season, and I want to be like them, to open my arms and float on
the supporting wings of expectation to whatever comes next. But
I cling to the branch of my old ways, long after I know that it is
not where I belong. I watch a chipmunk jumping and foraging,
darting about in a fine combination of playfulness and planning,
and I want to be like the chipmunk, enjoying my work for what
it is. But my need for security keeps me on guard and unable to
give myself to the moment for fear of sacrificing the future. I
admire the brilliant moon watchful of the night, and I want to be
like the moon, serene, present, and dependable. But my fear and
my longing keep me restlessly in motion and unable to give or
receive the love that the world knows.

Dear God who lives and works in human hearts and acts with
human hands, whose touch is on every fallen leaf, give me
strength to trust you. Let me remember in my darkest hours that
life is renewing itself in each moment and with that renewal
comes forgiveness and a fresh chance to try again. I am so
resilient to life's lessons at times when I ought to bow before
them, and so fragile at those moments when I ought to stand
strong.   Spirit of Life, I ask this morning that I may draw strength
from this place, this sacred space set among the fallen
leaves and the playful chipmunks, and beneath
the benevolent caress of the moon.

CONKER TIME

I picked up a horse chestnut Friday, right on the street in Cambridge near Harvard Divinity School.

Imagine that, a perfectly new horse chestnut. There were more for the picking had not my shyness and the stares of passersby prevented me from darting and pouncing to gather them up.

When I was a child, horse chestnuts were currency. Conkers, we called them. Better than a sixpence or even a shilling: a new conker had market value. Kids couldn't wait to harvest the green prickly cocoon with its polished mahogany prize. We'd climb the branches and knock the conkers off with a stick. No adult would've gotten near a bonanza like the one I found on Friday.

Funny the things we value: a new coat or a new car, a job that pays better, a best friend, or a good night's sleep. Me, I have always valued gifts from the earth. I hold this horse chestnut as I write about it. The warm brown nut fits my palm like a thumb in a baby's mouth, and the rich shiny skin gives my eyes something worthy of their sight. So I stare at it as if it were a crystal that could show me not the future, but the past; autumns of childhood
and wading in Wellington boots through rustling leaves
and playing with conkers on my
way home from school.

MOON PRAYER

Prayer and I were strangers once. But prayer called to me over the ocean, and I went to her in my good wool suit, high-heeled shoes, and a silk blouse that seemed to freeze on my skin. The waves said, "Shhh," as they explored my feet sinking in the wet sand, and I thought my part of the beach laughed that night to see me so strangely dressed for worship.

Not a boat was there, nor the cry of a gull, but stark winter branches pointing to the luminescent sky. I cupped my hands around the moon and kissed her and quietly pled my case: "I just came down tonight to see if the Creator had anything to say to me." Somewhere from its trundle bed my soul leapt into the mightiness of God-space and was caught up in the momentary foreverness of love, and I knew without understanding or needing to that the Creator had spoken.

THE PEBBLE

A smooth and rounded pebble rolled onto the beach with the last wave and was then lifted and swished back into the water. This happened over and over again until I could no longer tell which was the pebble I had picked out to watch from among the hundreds along that stretch of beach.

That is the way of pebbles—slow and unresisting. That pebble I watched may have been a mountain once, thrown up by the cracking together of continental plates a billion years ago. It may have been a boulder under the foot of a dinosaur and pushed south by the fingers of ice that stretched across Canada and down into the northern states during the Ice Age. It may have been used to hold the fire that warmed the hands of a Wampanoag tribeswoman.

This small smooth pebble may have been in the foundation stones of a pilgrim home or meeting house, and it may have been walked upon by the men and women who settled our towns and built our country. The pebble patiently accepts its formation by the weather and water, the attack of humanity, and the rounding that comes with the constant gentle caress of other pebbles as the centuries go by.

That is not the way of women and men. With our amazing array of ligaments, bones, and muscles, we are built for action and manipulation. With our brains and finely tuned senses, we are meant to conceptualize and create. It is given to us to work the earth and these pebbles, so we can change their shape rapidly and decisively. We are meant to move quickly and intentionally, to build up and knock down as we discover, and use our heads and hands to find meaning in our lives.

But perhaps the end is the same. In our fragmentary lives and
the pebble's long slow one, perhaps there is a design which
moves us both, people and pebbles, toward a smoothing off
inside; perhaps, in our effort to make sense of our existence,
we too are being rounded off, smoothed and polished
until our souls fit comfortably into
the mind of God.

MEDITATION FOR MARJORIE

I sit by your bed and hold your hand through the metal gate that guards you. Your body sealed into sleep looks disjointed, a jumble of bones haphazardly collected. Without its underlying layers your skin is translucent and fragile.

Outside, the last brittle and mottled leaves cling to the bones of a tree. I lean close and stroke your old head, but gently for fear I'll hurt you with my touch. I look at your skeletal frame with awe—the ultimate nakedness.

Another leaf silently slips through the fingers of bark and settles. Loss of vitality. The tree lets go of its leaves for its own survival. Its spirit lives on, buried deep in layers of fiber. Somewhere you are sleeping in the cradle of eternity. At last your tired eyes open and see me, and for a moment with marvellous surprise your dear face moves into the smile of joy and recognition. It is the impish smile of a little child; it is the smile of a beautiful girl, a lover's smile. I am drawn into the transitory mystery of your life and mine, and I almost forget to smile back.

The wind makes a move of defiance and scatters the remaining leaves. It is quiet; the tree weeps in silence and dignity, not in sorrow, but in hope. I think it is time to say good-bye.

LETTING GO

I went to the beach, and it was soft today, temperate hues merging and separating; clouds and ocean reflecting, complementing each other, and far away an occasional beam from the Gurnet Light.

Oh let me touch the faces of those I love with the same gentleness the waves show to the shore; let me sing my song with the same feeling with which the gulls fill the sacred space of sea and sky. Let me learn of beauty from the affection of morning sunlight; let my sorrow learn to meld with the tinted clouds; let my joy learn to swim and fly and fill the dawn with my delight.

And when my body is tired and no longer wants to be a part of
the active life, then let it be from here
that my soul flies free.

AND LET THE RIVER ANSWER

I went again to the mouth of the Bluefish River today. My heart was heavy; people I knew were hurting, some almost unbearably, and I couldn't help. How could I help others when I couldn't even help myself?

The sun hung elusive in an unwashed sky, and some water birds played tag in the chill river in defiance of the cold. The water lay still as if to dignify my sorrow, patiently receiving my story, respectful and nonintrusive.

Then inside me some old familiar words began to speak themselves: "Come unto me all you who labor and are heavy laden, and I will give you rest." I felt those words stir around me as the water eddied around the birds' feet.

I leaned against a stunted scrub pine at the edge of the water and closed my eyes. It was a comfort to know that the person who first spoke those words didn't have a particular idea in mind about what kind of burdens, or how heavy they should be, or where exactly we should go to lay them down, or what form our rest would take. It was left up to us to find our places of worship, to understand God in our own way.

The invitation was to trust that we were not alone, that we could share each other's burdens. And in the silence the river showed me how I could help.

UNTRIED WINGS

Hollow bones, streamlined feathers, and wings shaped to push aside the viscosity of air are not what make birds fly.

Birds let go of their grasp on safe perches at the tops of trees because something calls to them. They unfold their untried wings and feel an unimagined power. They soar out, up, and through the winter sky because an ancient longing pulls them home.

Loosed from the sticky grasp of earth, free from the snarls of lesser creatures with daggers in their teeth and muscles in their legs, birds laugh upward, homeward, drawn by a calling which bids them welcome in the sky.

Bird, take me with you when you go. Oh not my lumbering body and knitted tissue, no. Take some other me with you, some invisible soul of me that hears the call you hear, that moves effortlessly with you through the bright pink silk of dawn and the warm butter spread of morning. Carry my longing to be weight-
less, to move as light moves, to be unseen, scattered
through time and space. Teach me
to trust my wings.

ALL IS DUKKHA

"All is *dukkha*," say the Buddhists. I am told that *dukkha* is hard to translate. It means literally "suffering," but the feeling of *dukkha* is closer to impermanence; impermanence is central to the Buddhist path to nirvana, enlightenment.

Dukkha, all is impermanence, nothing lasts. I thought of that yesterday while watching leaves come down in a shower and inhaling the smell of rotting leaves returning to the earth. Leaf to humus and back to the earth to nourish the roots of the mother tree. The crows crying as the leaves fall and their nests are exposed—*dukkha*, all is impermanence.

Life goes by, and people who were with us last year at this time have died. All souls pass on, all is *dukkha*, nothing lasts.

The Buddhist path to enlightenment is understanding, accepting impermanence to the point where we no longer struggle against it. But here in the West we search for that which is permanent even as we live with ceaseless change and uncertainty. We search for a sure footing on the path strewn with fallen leaves; we notice the buds of next year's growth tightly curled and waiting; we hold on to the things we can count on: our church, our community, our memories of those who died before us, our love and hope, and our search for truth in a world that is *dukkha*.

Spirit of creation, Goddess of today—let us find each other in a changing world; let us experience love as something which exists, a possibility which is. Let us know that we are alive and being renewed miraculously each second; that the impermanence gives to life its freshness and surprise; that our memories of yesterday and our expectations of tomorrow make now a cherished, precious, eternal moment.

44

FOOTPRINTS

I stare out between the cold points of my coat collar, never noticing the periphery, intent only on negotiating the uncertainty of the snow-blown path.

Even the frozen earth seems to be on guard, tense against the slight of another thrust from the rapier air. Our houses creak and grumble, our cars itch with winter-thrown dirt, and even our own carefully nourished bodies feel as if the bones will fragment like icicles loosed from the roof.

But in my path lie the delicate footfalls of some creature who owns my yard, owns it every bit as much as I, but whose presence is betrayed only by the revealing snow. Who are you, little winter-coated traveler with the bare toes, too light to break through the layers of snowflakes, tracking this way and that in the moonlight, never daring to see if your fear of me is justified? These fragile prints sketched on the art-paper brilliance of the snow remind me that this parcel of land I call my own is really shared, leased temporarily from the rightful ownership of the natural world.

Slow me down, Spirit of Life, unfreeze my senses: Let me risk a little body heat to look from right to left to see the landscape in all its ice-laced loveliness and to touch my finger to the secret footprint of the nighttime traveler who
shares mysterious creation
with me.

SACRIFICE

The old tree standing in our yard saved someone's life today. We were preparing for the forecasted snowstorm, building a fire, planning a cozy day, and watching the first wild flakes when we heard an unmistakable sound. It was the sound of automobile-become-deathtrap, the sound of metal collapsing, cowardly, on impact. We called the police, fetched blankets, and hurried across the lot toward a folded car. It's nose was down, half buried amongst fallen branches and winter-exposed debris.

A man whose truck narrowly missed being in the car crash was already there, pulling open the passenger door. "Are you all right?" he asked to the young woman inside. He eased our blankets over her, and she shivered and nodded and didn't open her eyes. Quickly it seemed there were too many people standing around, needing to be where something bad had happened, needing to there and not knowing why.

The police and ambulance came and took her away. A wrecker towed the car, and at last the people dispersed. Did the driver of the truck want to come in the house? Was he all right? Yes, he was all right. He said "I'll go home, my wife is waiting for me."

The tree is in pieces. It gave its life. Had it not fractured and fallen when hit by the car, the girl might have died. In sacrifice it looks noble, as if it were part of something dramatic, like the saving of a life.

I don't know if I'm writing about a tree, a car crash, or about being scared. I think we were all scared out there. We said to each other: "She was lucky." But she was not. Had she been lucky, she would not have skidded off the road. She would not have known that sickening, paralyzing moment between out of control and impact. No, she's not all right. I hope tonight she has someone with her who understands that.

REFLECTIONS ON A PAINTING
BY ANDREW WYETH

In Andrew Wyeth's painting *Wind from the Sea*, the remains of a lace curtain blow in the wind from an open window. As I study the painting I see an abandoned cottage, maybe a summer home whose children have grown and moved away, maybe a house near a beach that has eroded. For whatever reason, the house is alone, and the picture smells of old curtains and sea breezes, and the tattered lace is all that is left of the draperies.

Sometimes we feel like that curtain—torn and fragmented, barely holding together, no longer providing either shade or decoration. Shredded, we feel, and abandoned, at the mercy of the wind.

But Wyeth shows us the whole picture. Look at the salt-bleached window frame. Touch its roughness, inhale the wind from the sea. Perhaps, says the painting, you are the window frame without a pane of glass to hold you back, without so much as a fingernail of paint to conceal your truth. Perhaps you are a window where the light streams in, through which the glory of morning and the changing of seasons may be seen. Perhaps, in the skeleton of lace and the stripped-down wood, there is honesty, no artifice, no pretense. Perhaps, after all, this cottage is not abandoned; perhaps it is a place to which seekers after truth come to find what is real and reliable, basic and honest.

The artist invites us, seekers after truth, to be both skeleton lace that is fragile, easily torn, and moved by the wind, and sturdy windows without glass through which the light shines. Thank you, Creative Spirit, for the artist whose genius gives us back ourselves, whose vision shows us who we really are, and whose art calls forth from us the hidden longing to be
understood and appreciated
just as we are.

THE CALL

I trod the heavy beach in winter. The wind insulted my face, and the ocean bared its white teeth, and I cried into the wind:

I am a person who wants to be mighty, but all too often I'm a grain of sand. I mean to blow strong across the ocean, but I never do more than ruffle the surface of the shallows. Sometimes I'm delighted with my uniqueness and my capacity for love, but then the hungry gull spies me and snatches me up and devours me. And then there is the anger...

There was no disembodied voice that day, only the warning cry of the gull; no bushes burned in my path, only the sunlight making fire in the water; no strangers bearing good news, no angels of the Lord. I was quite alone.

But then, somewhere inside me, there was a shift. One of those many little currents that link idea and action started rippling a little bit faster, and I imagined the voice of the Creator saying, "I'll take you as you are—fragile as the shell, irritating as the grain of sand, and unreliable as the wind—and I'll use you. Although your work will be impossible, like finding a perfect sand dollar, although you will be as abandoned as the beach in winter, although your reward will be the unforgiving beak of a hungry gull, I'll use you." And I walked on, filled with joy and gratitude.

HIGH TIDE, LOW TIDE

The bay at high tide is an invitation. It calls and I follow, falling into the chill wet blanket of motion and mystery. "Put down your face and stretch out," it sighs. "Relax, the element is friendly. Swim out to the raft and fill up your ears; hear the throb of the ocean massaging the land. Experience the momentary panic of salt water in your nose and mouth; go on, it's here for you." The bay at high tide is a sparkle of fiberglass and a slapping of halyards; it's a rolling, relentless sucking at the shore and uneasy toeholds on the backs of unseen sea creatures.

But at low tide the sand is strewn with the waves' forgotten favors. I stand, abandoned like one of the empty shells, staring out beyond the horizon where the water receded, where I cannot follow. Low tide is for reflection and acceptance. I do not belong to this water world after all. I long to wriggle into the muddy sand and shoot out tiny fountains like the clams, but I cannot. I can only stare into the pools from the salt-spray-softened surface of the beached raft and let memories bathe me.

There is a time for high tide—being involved and active, taking risks, and putting out effort to master the elements—and there is a time for low tide—inactivity and quiet reflection—and both are necessary in our lives. May this be a low-tide time for you, when you can hear the voice of your own calming and thoughtful inspiration, a time when thoughts come uncalled for to comfort or challenge you; and may you go from here renewed
and ready to answer the call of your destiny,
to jump back into the tide of life
once more.

UNITARIAN AND UNIVERSALIST
MEDITATION MANUALS

Unitarians and Universalists have been publishing annual editions of prayer collections and meditation manuals for 150 years. In 1841 the Unitarians broke with their tradition of addressing only theological topics and published *Short Prayers for the Morning and Evening of Every Day in the Week, with Occasional Prayers and Thanksgivings*. Over the years, the Unitarians published many volumes of prayers, including Theodore Parker's selections. In 1938 *Gaining a Radiant Faith* by Henry H. Saunderson launched the current tradition of an annual Lenten manual.

Several Universalist collections appeared in the early nineteenth century. A comprehensive *Book of Prayers* was published in 1839, featuring both public and private devotions. During the late 1860s, the Universalist Publishing House was founded to publish denominational materials. Like the Unitarians, the Universalists published Lenten manuals, and in the 1950s they complemented this series with Advent manuals.

Since 1961, the year the Unitarians and the Universalists merged, the Lenten manual has evolved into a meditation manual, reflecting the theological diversity of the two denominations. Today the Unitarian Universalist Association meditation manuals include two styles of collections: poems or short prose pieces written by one author—usually a Unitarian Universalist minister—and anthologies of works by many authors.

The following list includes all meditation manuals since the merger, plus most titles prior to 1961.

Unitarian Universalist

1992   *Noisy Stones* Robert R. Walsh[‡]

1991   *Been in the Storm So Long* Mark Morrison-Reed and
        Jacqui James, Editors[‡]

52

1961   *Parts and Proportions* Arthur Graham

Council of Liberal Churches (Universalist-Unitarian)

1960   *Imprints of the Divine* Raymond Hopkins

1959   *Indictments and Invitations* Robert B. Cope

1958   *Strange Beauty* Vincent Silliman

1957   *Greatly to Be* Francis Anderson, Jr.

1956   *My Heart Leaps Up* Frank O. Holmes

Unitarian

1955   *The Task Is Peace* Harry Scholefield

1954   *Taking Down the Defenses* Arthur Foote

1953   *My Ample Creed* Palfrey Perkins

1952   *This Man Jesus* Harry C. Meserve

1951   *The Tangent of Eternity* John Wallace Laws

1950   *Deep Sources and Great Becoming* Edwin C. Palmer

1949   *To Take Life Strivingly* Robert Killan

1948   *Come Up Higher* Hurley Begun

1947   *Untitled* Richard Steiner

1946   *The Pattern on the Mountain* (reissue)
          E. Burdette Backus

1945   *The Expendable Life* Charles G. Girelius

1944   *The Disciplines of Freedom* Leslie T. Pennington

1943   *Faith Forbids Fear* Frederick May Eliot

1942   *Forward into the Light* Frederick W. Griffin

1941   *Victorious Living* W. W. W. Argow

1940   *Address to the Living* Herbert Hitchen

1939   *The Pattern on the Mountain* E. Burdette Backus

1938   *Gaining a Radiant Faith*   Henry H. Saunderson

Universalist

1955 *Heritages* Harmon M. Gehr

1954 *Words of Life* Albert F. Ziegler

1953 *Wisdom About Life* Tracy M. Pullman

1952 *Spiritual Embers* John E. Wood

1951 *The Breaking of Bread* Raymond John Baughan

1950 *Add to Your Faith* Roger F. Etz

1949 *To Take Life Strivingly* Robert Killam

1948 *Of One Flame* Robert Cummins

1947 *Using Our Spiritual Resources* Roger F. Etz

1946 *A New Day Dawns* Walter Henry Macpherson

1945 *Beauty for Ashes* Robert and Elsie Barber

1944 *The Price of Freedom* Edson R. Miles

1943 *The Ladder of Excellence* Frank D. Adams

1942 *The Whole Armor of God* Donald B.F. Hoyt

1941 *Earth's Common Things* Max A. Kapp

1940 *The Interpreter* Frederic W. Perkins

1939 *The Great Avowal* Horace Westwood

1938 *Add to Your Faith* Roger F. Etz

‡ These meditation manuals are available from the Unitarian Universalist Association. For a free catalog, write to the UUA Bookstore, 25 Beacon St., Boston, MA 02108-2800.